L

Letters to Unfinished J.

Sheila E. Murphy

Winner of The Gertrude Stein
Poetry Award 2001

GREEN INTEGER
KØBENHAVN & LOS ANGELES
2003

GREEN INTEGER
Edited by Per Bregne
København / Los Angeles

Distributed in the United States by Consortium Book
Sales and Distribution, 1045 Westgate Drive, Suite 90
Saint Paul, Minnesota 55114-1065

(323) 857-1115 / http: // www.greeninteger.com
lilycat@sbcglobal.net

This edition first published by Green Integer in 2003
10 9 8 7 6 5 4 3 2 1

Some of these poems previously appeared in the journals *Disturbed
Guillotine, Happy Genius, Lost and Found Times, Poetry New York,
Talisman, Transmog, Vigil, The Vision Project, Way* and *Wooden Head
Review*. The author wishes to thank the editors of these publications.

Cover: Photograph of Sheila E. Murphy
©2002 by Beverly Carver
Design: Per Bregne
Typography: Kim Silva

LIBRARY OF CONGRESS CATALOGING IN PUBLICATION DATA
Sheila E. Murphy [1951]
Letters to Unfinished J.
p. cm — Green Integer: 93
ISBN: 1-931245-59-X $10.95
I. Title. II. Series.

Green Integer books are published for Douglas Messerli
Printed in the United States of America on acid-free paper.

for Beverly Carver

I.

Episodes leave milk in warm looking containers. Trees hover with the just-right looking attitude we teach children to emulate, spelled e-m-u. *I come from the Midwest where sheep often in rows still seem as random as the growth in pasture.* Minions in the form of attitudes keep passing dawn and other chapters lengthwise with attention to their width. Big looking apparatus confers the status of price-value on machinery, a kind of economic Peyton Place with dots for pins in map face. The risen Christ is central to dogmatic lack of mountains. *(See: Variation.) Why don't you just go home and manufacture knots.* A music box reality, let us recall, is repetition always tempting to the wall we have constructed for appearance of delirium. Some gifts need to be chanted for effect. Local merchants have achieved a status that deflects agreed-upon childhood. *Try and tell an elder something.* Lullabies are popular because we've saved them for the last dark window of the day.

2.

Whatever sifts us we have traced to mother lodes
no neighbor will refine. When I go to stretch my
legs the partial wilderness leaves me dramatic as
suburban woods with interruptive homes in
them. Like mapdots blinking tiny festivals
across. The thief as first perceived by innocents,
fails to resemble selves. No more than one ounce
of pardon can remain for him. Supplies not plen-
tiful leave space for rumination. And the cost of
energy supplants the energy itself. Remaining
envy pricks the seedling he has breathed upon to
alter any syndrome linked to growth. Appease-
ment would replace a litany that otherwise
would flow. Address systems pour luminarias
into equations where we'd bask our fright away.
Drop a fleck of silver on the downtime thought
to be mercurial for some, rubato for the rest.
How often do you listen to the Pope in native
tongue. And what of the vernacular can learn to
breed you. *She was so prim and corporate, the
usually rebellious one feared being capsized.* I
heard her talking to herself about the difference

between current tasks and those reserved for morning. When the show has passed what will we have given to the centuries. A malted would be nice.

3.

He had a melted cheese look in his eye. I wanted
then to touch but we were housed in our official
stances making gestured conversation. He had a
lift poised in his shoe. Each one of us interpolat-
ed who we thought we were along fair lanes I
memorized the turf war and released it. Return-
ing to the child who told boys where to stand
along the football field. For the first time I saw
light as a perfume within his eye. Two forms of
inattention. Now my mind is waltz prone. Now
I'm ready for earned relaxation. Wash made
ready on the line, the milky tones of birds, the
small velocity of cinders when a car drives up.
The way his after shave chimes knotty pine.

4.

Teach me to be a Polish cook who's fluent in the spices and can fashion taste in nourishment. My home perspires boredom with the instant things I pass off as planned meals spawned by skin-of-teeth arrivals up a driveway separate from *plaisir*. Teach me to factfind buttery mementos of long afternoons pronouncing French between delectable taste copings that rescind all disciplined approaches to consumption. I want to talk. I want to harbor urges that won't wait. Let me be Irish in another way. Twirl on the tongue most active verbs replenished by something *garni*. I'm mad with my incapability near false starts toward culinaria. I want to cook for you a sit-still menu we can lounge before and taste and recommend some spoken passages relating to . . . Teach me to make saurbratten when you're well enough to eat it. Teach me quiche. Teach something Florentine remanding Popeye to involuntary punches held close to the chest. This house, a spice rack in your majesty's subconscious. Sit beside me, we'll both talk. About meals to be defined by need and satisfying crumbs as leavened as the risen glide toward sanctity observed and rumored more than actual. My place is at the farm habitually swollen with the fullness of grown things. Bushels of them waiting to be bountiful in other forms.

5·

In a little while I will be wanting to neglect something. Within my grasp, long noise of yawning. Sibilants and cheese and saucy looking pie prints enter the confessional. Instinct reminisces prettily. Prawns fully formed elicit feedback on legions of eighth notes aspiring to be whole tones. Ministers of holographic space warm the confetti pool before it's tossed into small pits without immunity to ridicule. All coughing noise lacks balance, taste, and gentian violet. Piracy infects the tear ducts. Pluck and whimsy brighten claustrophobia. Promise me you'll toss a world my way, negotiable as skin. That's my mood on diction. Same thing as the water and the jar, inseparable. Twin reeds play at tethering known melody until it frills the place with overtones. What are monikers equipped for. Achievement of a breakpoint. The rhetoric accomplishes this "waves of grain" behavior. All of us swaying to breezes *understood as grammar.* Perfectly informed. Perfectly splintered. How handsome seeds are likely to become. What hasps these instants are. What bread.

6.

It is possible to unlearn all arithmetic except
subtraction. Need more time to savor what is
posh or not. She specialized in deals inversely
proportional to guilt that blocked them. *A prolif-
ic nature has been frequently accustomed to the
quintessential blotter that discourages continu-
ance and ironical enjoyment of a thing.* The
mindless sitcom root canals worthy pursuits. I'm
lit up like halogen over some surrogate remark.
Need plainsong or desert minus Marlboros.
Bunches of news promote a frenzy of granules
spun into a clever spate of breath. Remind her
not to tell me what they talked about in bed. I
don't practice forging intimate connections.
Parks are never neutral places, just reputed to
be so. What is the procedure to make cherished.
Easily the room around us, having forfeited co-
incidence especially opaque as we now know it.
What is therapy. Therapy is the supreme being
who made all things. Do you have need of ink, if
so, how often. *This is the way we spend our
dimes* . . . In rhymes, a primitive enjoyment.

7.

We had been actively comparing cabooses. The more overall our world, the more conformist, and the less full-figured bliss there was to go around. We watched somebody ostracize just once *for fun*, amid snares of doubt clobbered by one rumored to be wise. The leg meld of signatories retained what had seemed best among the spoils left to departing urchins. No one picks nuns to serve on teams. If and when the chaperone stops yawning I'm investing in a plot. The cost of living smells like moving to the avenues where people strive like reflexes that someone should disown. Whatever caliber we have renounced will scream the kinds of platitudes that lift the dead from all their boredom. Lace does to a woman's face what leaves do to the branches of an oak. Commerce lingers in our memory. Whatever tumult cannot last we resurrect. Having pieced together sanctions, we strive to form erasers that conform to specs. What do books advise. The small humidifier in the bedroom clips the act of coughing prior to its chest of drawers' arrival. Put another way, the only beads of moisture that we know about exude from skin. The off-white morning in a motel proves that nothing happens in this world save daytime reruns. All attempts to defrost someone's line of credit are denied. Life positioned to resemble a simplicity we cannot learn without signed papers and assurances. The only limber act of God is locked up in a mainframe.

8.

Theater is part-way bald. You wouldn't like her
heritage until she asked. The press of newlywed
economy stands to inhibit ripe old sagebites
tuned to weld one forest to the next. The name
Yolanda stiffens. Maybe too much vowel too
soon. Hyperbole unlocks intensity for one good
stroll around the leeward avenues. My comb is
threadbare and my name delays its walkmarks in
your yard. You noticed, too, the ritornello and
the sirens shaping what they shape. You have to
listen to them unglue surfaces before we're
numb. Before we're centered into the fast
ground ball, groundswell, ground breaking parl-
ance. What can we associate from blamed green
carpet. Reach precedes grasp unless we're all the
way seamed into lawns like petit fours. Accoun-
tancy smells like an honor so the spoils increase
lacking savority. Mere mention of enslaved dis-
posal halts our nameplates from deserving what
we scribe. False flutterings. We feed our tame
brew something. We allow ourselves to be an in-
step from denial. And in retrospect stupidity

means something people pay to free from the usurpive role. F-sharp is able to break glass in the hand. Barometers don't measure flings. Line item lovenest quakes when there is something beyond breeze passing the items on a clothesline back and forth as indecision handles part of what it knows.

9.

We want so much to earn a common dialect but syllables emerge identical instead. Pump out the spine if no stomach is available. "Translate your mother's womb and call me in the morning." That's what the professor said in answer to the first question that formed a mind. An invigorating speech impediment unclouds probable distance. Flaws tumble before the grill of third-hand Oldsmobiles, always stalled at signs that have lost color. She made up a life, transcribed it upon sheets he'd be the first to tell you are inadequate. There but for the rendezvous went petty thieveries of solitude. Which one achieved first fluency without an artificial other. Which one sieved the rivered forms of dress. She wanted to eavesdrop on unspilled prose. Cameo appearances housed among keepsakes outside the stream of correspondence. How do we communicate if shaking hands becomes the sole available mistake.

10.

She withdraws from all that I pronounce. Windows repeat the clear skin of a flowered tree. *Explain momentum.* Spiritus sanctus gesturing. It did not seem that she would leave according to the clock. We held our eyelids open toward the coming of unnamed birds lingering with stranded melody. How narrow is an atmosphere. The field glow after census. How beautiful can data be. One lark after another unlike profit motive. Near our grasp with adverbs archived. Shallow pool collective noun. Awaiting the return post evidence of mind and light affection. Minuet dissolves into a download fashioned to seem memorable. Thin lapse of morning's scenic sleep. The trees gesture with meaning we assign. Elastic hinges near a rumination. She rehearsed her cherishing mid-winter. Each page of the diary recurs perhaps unmeasured. Natural fecundity commandeers elision. A transom to have crossed. On hold the lumen yanks a twig out of regressive loam. An auditory frost returns the serve timely as mass. Collects whatever might live fruitfully on rosters. Vegetation. World prayer affords us memory. Her first depression stays awake throughout the night. Interiors eventually collapse. Are shared. Recur. Words clinging to concepts lapse. Identifiable detention swells thanklessly enough to warrant some of the supposed branches. Dark full walls connect with light. Vouchsafe and church the softest of amenities. So simple the mushroom under a shade tree. What she said was you're so busy and you've called me. Misunderstanding carte blanche. Puncture wounds eventually fill in differently from wish. To feel not just observe the bloom. Become the bloom. Subsumed into the everlasting permanence of bloom.

II.

Blanket frayed with woolballs, raspy threads so in the night his comfort pales. I watch the bed a moment before wisping past some hopeless pairs of eyes that have been caught. So many men sleep in this small space under different blankets. Dust paced to mean behavior in disintegrating sunlight. Sheets of it in drawers retained like photographs. Limitations lose percussion one by one. He wrote to say ethereum within my sentences included no trap door, no front door, no basement window. Everything on paper was a map to peacetime. While immersed in using the machines that held the possibility of making me seem beautiful. How we pounce on the return key. Game plan not agreed upon. He told me that when energy is scarce he thinks in small steps and decides upon proceeding from one morsel to the next. Hair length not to be trusted. Arbitrary to the touch. Some pair of beads residual releasing passion once removed. Whose clothes are these blue, darker blue to easily identify transgression from the several

moments or half lifetime prior to a natural mis-
take. Branded with a rational response supposed
to seem a system. Whole swatches of experience
seeming dated as the intersection of realities.
Blue ice failing to include a country to the north
where it is rumored to be cool.

12.

A caterwaul makes cool injustice. *Hear what we are living* out of sequence following small sugared pieces of hysteria. The osmotic freelance pastor deft with pliers cranked an engine into bliss. For now, the ruminative flurry tends to slather on intemperate myopia. For whose sake. Aspertame is not delicious without salt. Body chemistry indulges in recidivism. Ankly young girls t.p. someone's house. A boyfriend matters. Who incites presumptive rioting beneath the inseam of adoptive parenting. Notes abide by rules. Contraltos hide fatigue in friendship. When we close our jaundiced eyes the ritual comes back to proctor tests on tapestry. *I imagined leaves a little dry this time of year though drenched with scent that offered a migration.* House sitters often plentiful become slow worms. What would the doctor have to say about a temperature we thought was lost. See what is hanging on the line fail to engulf the antibodies anymore. *He held out his hand and I was sure of an impending death.* At such a moment prayer becomes a zither whose own strings will be forgotten.

13.

Soprano cuts of her first album water half my
plants. I dram a sheaf of little wind for motion to
alive me. Seashore sunrooms all the plexiglass I
know. The view is tantrum. And the lithe phan-
tom of how we bake love slyly paces across the
logic of indigenous pale flowers. Cushions in
our memory come due. We prance across Sch-
enectady. We softball our collective conscience.
We leave a fleck of room in sylph land to have
practicum and talk unto the hour of candles. At
the grotto all the prayer we have mirrors each
handpicked stone. What are others praying for.
The woman who immerses who she is in play-
things paused a moment while we softened like-
ly outcomes with cool voice. The secret of ad-
miring plants she'd sprinkled and could save.
The secret of accepting how things stop and
what is left, inevitable embrace. With slow
hands true as souls that would release as many
things as they have grasped. One phase at a time
until the integration. Final as the color pale in
an uncertain sky. Locales have seasons and lo-

cales enroll in our affection. One time and an-
other to form patterns that will be there after
anyone can reach us anymore.

14.

Fugues are part of us. The woven semblances of lamb and then soft space to try on hammockly. She thought retention and the music as a feast. The hurt from El Dorado happiness much like her having painted over raw wood instead of sanding, priming, fixturing what was to be. The moment thought embeds itself in mind there is a physicality. *So let us pray, she symptoms and caresses evidence of swaying trees.* Some leisure of a kind of field with crops to be untied she wistfully communicates in letters. *Things left unsaid made holy.* To a brother she depicts emotions left to other selves, pries shelf dolls from the nest. The limber eloquence of barbed wire crosses branches against windows that have framed her talking near a smitten tree. *They came directly from the game in clothes designed for approbation.* Minutes had been taken and then kept. A prerecorded chapter left to dry. The weaving we at last perceived in strands while moving far beyond them.

15.

He half elbowed his way out of the frost. We were unmutually not enemies, no cost was exacted, every ritual you name was represented in notetaking moderato with a chaperone who sent a wire from God reminding us of our fetality long since expired. It was production season. All the lateral impassives gonged together noose points to retract the weariness of sin and its remaining ointment. We rowed to match old inclinations. Rivers stowed their stasis. Homogeneous intentions ricocheted off pyramids. Someone was hovering above the hasp connecting everglades and promising intentions. Power clothes hung on to voiceprints while the pen riled every surface of legality. No glowering came from whipstitch centers to the right and left. We fathomed ourselves apolitical, and he could dream, sit up, take nourishment by his own hand. I was an economy. Cobbled sweets were limned along Formica. He spoke without coffee about systems. In crisp tie, reminisced traditional intaglio, the lack of menacing equality, exacting value-neutral neural nines, rotomontade of cherishing.

16.

Tone row bears no burden of familial links to clog the metaphoric arteries. Though Berg antennaed passion in a tremble of a way through intervals tasting of pattern. Violins made to sound like touch in debt from borrowed feeling. So elision tufts a modest effort toward the snow. *No leaps sanctioned* no Winnebago from points on map to fire. Relationships among discrete things formed magnetic norms in context of the light. The tenor voices treason playground bars with all they want to grow. A cinch in temperature removes homeopathic *like* from threat of cure. *People exist exactly where they are, people desist, people appropriate lives of their own . . .* To hear the thought of passion undertongued by brevity is close to myth declaring music *actually crafted* not drawn free style like the fish commodity through ponds. Malt of intelligence slides farther than a planned direction west. Snow ethically ransoms winter. *Screen calls without prossessive adjective.* Listen to a random wasp be the remote thread. Watch wired nest.

Interrogate the closet selfish fixture who insists on sanctity. Conferral ranks toward top of the triangle too dry to enjoy. *Franchise on guilt hovers within the instrument until a residue of song is given thus erased thus falsified* . . . Jim dandy little cordless phone you're bragging on. At last count, portions of land still traipsable remain alert to tension. Continue miming strength until eyes glisten with the yield of an intelligent contagion.

17.

She listed her hobby as disclosure. Many of the new remarks unfolded as she pressured silence to relax its throat hold on her policies. One of the immaculate new moods undressed a neighbor's eloquence. He was so beautiful at once I categorized approximate undoing wink by wink until he'd talk to me. Suspicious looking avenues were few to the timetables anyone arranged. Bright colored ivy nonsensed every living caustic rue in Paris. No one melodied with more finesse than she whom I would veto on the sticking point of cabins with excessive room. Why were there suitcases positioned in the textured park. Whose cameras were these fortifying nature as gestured to the tune of leavened peaks and dune mass landed in the cove we used to occupy. The conversation was mimetic. Anything I grasped, soon discarded. What is it to be comrades, to seem strong enough for sandwiches to carry you as far forward as there are permits. Lucre on the shelves was painted shades of craft. One of the falsehoods I unraveled was a synonym for gravity.

18.

Transactions crease themselves into a careful frenzy. Would we wash the photograph, air the detritus with film versions of a novel loved for all its quiet. Sitting uninterrupted. Do prime leaves want to coast and do prime leaves occur. Anybody's guess accustoms us to trinkets forced and competent, conceived of as the nature tolerant of courses. Volume bantered in the broken weeds. Accustomed to the weeds and sentences. A ladder man assigns his trade to our few branches. Leaves have fallen. Leaves beneath the window. All we might have thought, frustration of enduring complication after . . . With a meld of force and waiting, something exists to be observed. Watch what is available. A scenery the same as breeze the same as old clairvoyance. The man who customizes small tasks to our recollection acts as though he hears what is between branches and leaves. The most that we could hope for. Listening like that to mimic what he knows, but not discovering. We sit together in the photograph perhaps again. Our clothes as soft and comfortable as leaves allowed to age as they have fallen.

19.

The power of distraction softens what is fixed. *Discernment of casual from well-defined causality attained status of art.* We were fed discrete low meals of voice. Opinions milded by. Revision macrobiots its way onto my chart, to be updated hourly as the bishop wishes. Say thank you to the sport forgiveness. Fossilarity comes to taunt recent hypotenuse. Meandering frost thieves consummate desires of any regiment. *As the good man whispered by I thought less of his competence than linkages between containment and extended breath.* What are we together for in this bright beatnik neighborhood. Viscosity comes true. *I notice words not learned before the age of twenty-five resist an occupation of the mind.* Lightbulb with pink scent owns scant restitution. Camera-ready feeling instigates small unpainted out takes. And copyable fee programs reduce themselves in size *within the text*. All day one spent attention inside the garage. All day the other spent attention in the reading room. Collaboration had in common with itself the absence of the word "pounce." City afternoon's reason for being. A nose flute state of the economy. Religious reasons to alert fractions of breath.

20.

Horn players resent the genericity that leaves the mist off instruments. The shimmer of insolvency. The brawn of remade brakes. There goes random brass again as if disqualifying constancy of a percussion leading everything that breeds. Specks of loquacity spurn tumblers of perked Baldrige. Whose org. is it anyway, whose heat, the thought of mewn hybrids first soft. Some of Arizona's wheat. Grass. Hemp. And sideways clover. Bandages with blood on the exact plant. Vast sums leave their coffers. So residents ingest the scent of silver. Warmer pearls. Riced features new to glaring postured eyelids. Here alone within the room. A note destroyed to crusted glass. Death by Prague disrobes before the sleeved accompanists enlisted for eternity.

21.

He's so smart that I remembered I might love him. Planets ditsed into a mai tai that I had to disinfect. Performed somnolent basket weave on my file manager in the spirit of spring cleaning. The most brilliant man I know can't function. It's one-stop mopping after him where I don't care to live. Meanwhile, the matriarch moons on about unhappened things I had forgotten. Confetti used to be derived from something whole. My plate of rice is littered with Parmesan in lean strips partly melted. Policy dictates steps shaped like a cream-based waving flag. Prance seems any likely posture when the field is blond in character and lumpen near the postured weeds. I heard Mr. Intelligent recite a recipe I treasure from afar where we dissolve into gratuities afforded unnamed creaks in posture, lanky code, and snarled specifics. He and I would clash I've stated hypothetically on more than one occasion. Diaries are full of this, and then I burn them. It didn't take me long to gather up amnesia like a wildflower bouquet to heal peculiar longing from which a recovery transcends unlikelihood. He's known for what he carries in a pail held far from his left side. Air reputed to be nothing is much more. He has explained it thus in terms equivalent to grief specifically my own.

22.

Sleep, although plush, cannot be recognized
within scrapbooks scented like libraries dressed
in fine feathers of dust. She wore her glasses
long upon the nose, and fibrillations manicured
the stop loss of her headache. The market lives
to be manipulated. Allows malarkey to unfasten
ribbons that uncover: plash and withered snap-
shots of spoons worth more than reflex. Pressed
lamp softens with the color pink our made up
minds that face the neighbors. Frost lures us to
a place where plaque will be less noticeable to
spines. How much can bodies bear with minds
so very like them. Circumspect arrangements
flow as winter perched above a Bunsen burner.
Given irresemblance to familiar moments
waltzed into a world of free throw lines consid-
ered tangent to imagined wilderness.

23.

Yard sales divest collectives of ingredients still joined. A coloring book divulges a child's feelings about plantedness, the scent of roots, their impact on the molten ground. One buyer following the next constructs timetables in association with connective commerce, tissuing the blessings of an arbitrary South. *A community in what sense serves its members.* Neighbors stand randomly in rows we sportingly misunderstand. A truce seems momentarily in vogue before adjournment. Senators emerge from ranks like these. Tourniquets and on-ramps become tools. A scapular negates the need for modules that explain illogic of some remedy agreed upon therefore believed. One of the livable redemptive sectors asks for bathing money to transpose arrangements. *She emitted secrets from a place beneath her breath.* Most of the morning coffee coexisted with a conversation labeled "good." Blushingly the sky yawned silver treblemarks. The loose shirtwaist of woodland traced a fall. The latency erected states of mind whose residue would turn out to be vast, inseparable from lumens. The reflexology of unnamed shards half gray. Earnings tap their mildest rays by soft association. Sinecures remain the earth of dreams. Replenish losses catalogued by reputation. One and then another.

24.

Tapioca linkages pop little suffocations. It is mothlike in the cubicles. The sugar that remains intrudes on otherwise distilled and fragrant mood. The pierced wood owns so many holes. And daily I receive books in the mail from someone who perceives my shell to be as permanent as I am. On TV the anachronistic man stout in his gray suit points at places having weather. Voice not meant for dueling vindicates the see-through resurrection someone powerful can know or at least think. A white lab coat connotes a form of expertise that does not touch. Comedians are rarely bland. They like to *be* us just enough to capture an attention. Wings unridden trace the lines toward anybody's pulse. Economy is sparsely flavored noontime. Seamed centrifugality wends its way home lacking in caretake. Brisk small shadows quake thereafter. When she works productively she hums and alternately carries on a conversation with herself. For all we know, wind can be turned down like a coping mechanism. Frilled with flavor stand-alone and lined with gratitude. Counting things assumes the rigor of reality half-tantalized into remote neglect. Lackluster phonographs rescind all latticework we hold like cirrus clouds. Anyone forgivable is half past rain. So say the sentences embedded in our least romantic curfews.

25.

Decorum wafts into the semicircle, searching for
an opening more subtle than the arc made by the
letter "J." The room is cluttered with recovery.
Stories leave a tarnish reminiscent of ashen
thumb paintings on foreheads. *Describe an out-
ward sign and its effects.* Participants arm wrestle
lines into a yeast of artificial touch. Each be-
haves as though instructed to French kiss a mir-
ror. *Parades cost money. Lives cost money. Chil-
dren . . .* She gathers would-be blooms into her
arms but not her heart. Lectures them and some
who might be listening or premising a likeness to
their private histories. Down in the street, traffic
and crowd scenes perspire blood. *There is a fee
for marching outside a democracy.* Plea bargain-
ing erupts into a hedge against emotional infla-
tion. *Trust is a mood-altering drug.* All evenings
end with pantomime of willed transcendence.
Too precisely wanted by the ravenous who long
to matter to a universe that seems not to have
mattered back.

26.

Every day we're reasonable and every day we're twice as blond as grain responding to the wind tongue. Lappily pronouncing weather like arpeggios within some pre-determined boundaries made and published and then sounded. With the fervor of a flag waved in the confines of eternity. Bright material subtracts itself from paths connecting what is natural with what is maimed. Seldom-hardened leaves unfasten a presumed allegiance to the trees. We camera our way to floral things removing silhouettes. The only widening of winter seizes any vest we name. As ravishing as plums against white sheet prepared for painting where immortality becomes a stiffness melodied apart from shadows. Breeding tumult the way humor czars its way to status of a thumbnail.

27.

Fingers in pie (blackbirds). My mentor was a mood to me, a priest, a humid wash of possible stilettos somewhere in the evenstance. Who introduced the possibility of circumspection by first speaking the word, referring to someone with photos in his left breast pocket we presumed. As yeast implants the further possibility of chances rising. With quicksilver light and certitude, of summer's moderato. It had not before occurred to me to hide fruits that I told myself would spoil if not consumed. Imagining the pocket where a tiny stain implanted shadow evidence of something now evolved to worthlessness. I had not perceived the mathematics of withholding. Observed the gleam within a negative, as silent as a tease. Diminishing to yield first picture that might have cloned original intent, if correspondence equaled trust, if time did not invite manipulations to complete the full equation.

28.

Poise occurs without the threat of anything's extinction. Threes are tossed like amulets into a fevered conversation texturing one skin against another. *When we spend time with them we lumber into accents not our own but comfortable.* The house becomes as quiet as a personality. Then nuisance variables begin to spark. Rain clatters on tin things and rattles windows. Only with no noise is there acceptance. *Tomorrow she departs the house for the last time.* How closely do emotions follow tasks. Beseechive sadnesses ask more than they would want. Ask less. What will be offered past the flowers. What are the names of flowers. What flavor has been wanted. The easily let go moments prompt resourcefulness of self to bathe anew environments of each day. Promptly, surely, visibly. Until no body notices the flagstones to be walked upon. These planted skipping stones without a lake or river to have bathed them.

29.

Time invested in the ones called worthless *proves something*. A way we might trade spiritual binoculars for reading glasses to *inspect the face, our own*. We take for granted peacetime and find little wars to place in it. The hate shield follows. Compassion on empty, an impossible quirk. What could he have been thinking when he sliced a sample of humanity. *Only profound percussion that gets implanted can make possible salvation less a wafer in the mind.* Love indefinitely postponed. Reciprocity from which we don't recover, but endure. *She pantomimed love until she felt it* without labeling. He began as he was nearing last awareness to give back the kind of dry arrangement of spent flowers she could live on. Watered by reflex given, not commanded. Part of the misted frame surrounding *what is possible*. What might persuade us to give up our shields, our power to delete what likely would splinter us. *The belief in a connection.* Soil to flower.

30.

Practice touch became a specialty. Consider rings of light barely approachable. *La meme chose* considering the circumstance. She finds herself propped up in confort with the air-conditioning. As vagueness settles-in importantly. And prompt new crayons fortify some space left by our wondering on empty what might have the nerve to seem new. Focusing rescinds the only doubt we know to orchestrate as little tufts of velvet seem shown in the hothouse of perspiring uncles looking with intentions. Some odometers seem often lame. Some shorelines promise to be natural. Some breakneck speeds seem quite pedestrian. The livery inspects itself beneath the watchful supereye of provosts profiled to seem gods we watch for down the hall. Real touch real time encourage trespassing on a chigger of reality whose cool pearl viaduct approximates the lovely neck of someone sought. Precision stings the sense of downtime for inadequate hewn seedlings. Hope's a funny animal whose fur becomes a predicate as often as we're named a proxy in this legal coach house near the lake. Obligation echoes obbligati if you play a keyboard often. Instrumental lingering detracts from vocal instability. Our housing resurrects a sense of play, fall colored in the spirit of arrest. The silo seems half full of ricotta recommended by a friend. We channel portions of a utilized IQ believing a rebuilt thing is consistently of higher caliber than something newly minted, spit-shined, perfectly unstained.

31.

Seldomness elapsed the washed glands more than strategy would prompt. *She requested that I pray her energy would saunter back.* The putty near tub's optimum interior. *I do what I am told almost.* Prose hinged twice around parfait of sure resemblances aligned with all the motor pool that craft allowed. DeSotos at a craft fair. Spare tire plus four. Rubbed keepsake, fast response. The automatic sanctioning. Political seamed craft we nouned ourselves into, cool southern intellect that fostered othering. *So what if he's not here. What difference did it ever make to have him held fast to the borrowed scent of winter.* Satchels of remembered heat noosed all the way to gather points. Rat fur as surrogate for the synthetics. The shiver that accompanied alternatives was often parallel to ripe sun glistening still mimesis of interiors. *The story told of gathering fruit to make a project of preserving flavor at the point of ripeness.* He glommed onto the opportunity to blue line fame. The trepidation that was in effect contagious forged a see-through category fashioned into faith. A random custom warranted loose nails like that. Circumference and trill. *Sequester.*

32.

We ought to have been steeped in summer with
arrangements as we preached whatever nose-
bleed had been logged into a book. No mysteries
took time to exist. He was better looking with a
palm over his eyes so we could read deflected
thoughts lodged in a kettle waiting to go off. Es-
tablishing that opposites retract. The limit of
our falsehood shared its store of prefixes. We
held a pair of cameras ready to have confiscated
any likely jury. Talked over small and large
events. We turned them inside out, or left them
where they were. Each afternoon imagination
transposed numbers in my favorite temperature.
The hibiscuses don't sleep. We find them preen-
ing from indulgent looking goalposts. Does it
matter what we know has mattered often. The
woman who wore several pairs of glasses every
week became a tintype dressed brown as a Fran-
ciscan. Cement fields border who we are. A fine
white gold machine. With lavender appoint-
ments southerly in their finesse.

33.

My penance is to capture what I said I wanted
and to feel it inches from my heart years follow-
ing the loss of interest. Practicum elicits me. *To
rid her of extraneous dance perhapsive.* Wearing
the loose whisper of Chanel. Delay is not the
hair part of a princess. Never mind her precious
evocation thus erasure of timetables. Impersonal-
ity bedraggles an antiphonal art form. Ques-
tions run dimly through the surcharged night.
The worthy tea. The stricken tea. Mood water of
repeated nights that sample hesitation till it's
useful to a memory. What glance becomes mere
undesired percussion. I tire of the unwanted ges-
tures. Shrink from accidental touch. Become the
board I was when dating in the reproductive
years I passed with gratitude. *Will she grow prac-
tical if I refrain from watching.* How soon will
fullness of alone time rinse my arms with a deli-
cious shadow. Making the complaining noise of
one not fluent in batons, keyboards, or fountain
pens.

34·

We salsa-ed halfway home. Snowshoes encrust-
ed with a certain form of dust. As managers of
pencil shavings left their posts to sneeze a
Wabash sneeze collectively. It has been fun one
told me before bungee jumping off a logo cir-
cling remnants of the sky. What if we did not
have to work, what would we wear through sleep
and Soho. Were we branded in the womb I won-
der, were we sleeves for someone curvy as a pool
cue's edge. Were we invested in school colors
critical as blue along somebody's hemline. How
many dramas do we have to like before being
residual. I like those blame-free code words lit-
tering my path. I like equally the pre-fab houses
caked with mud and featherings. We want our
sofas to be wood. Our birdhomes to be lumi-
nous. Our cue cards to seem weathered as a
supple link. The broom went by another quarter
of this ritual. And seed pods helped us reminisce
our fate. Test venerated corpulence for one and
lean bones for another. Confident of being
sipped by wounded angels.

35.

She promised herself not to seem confused
when someone talked. Marigolds just now in
bloom beside the window. Still easy to count.
The possibility of no more rain. Whatever has
been pieced together by the sky approximates an
early morning confiscation of the few pale eggs
still broken after wind. She promised to exert the
effort of a prayer with the finesse of crayon.
Summer with its inclinations last to know. Some-
one who functions. Equally someone who cares.
The roller blade of symptoms sleeks across ar-
cades. And quintessential humor in the heart.
What time did the meeting half begin. She
thought she would discuss this fraction of her
health. And it was morning then again with im-
ages sharp, unstrained. She was a camera once
and sang the blisters of falsetto. She totalled
what she'd earned and monks as customers had
offered to resign for her. The hammock trimlined
to mean luxury was coming. She was third and
losing strength while finding rungs she did not
feature nor install in crevices of memory. The lit-

tle that she knew for certain lip-synched words someone had written to be salt without the threat of water or of fire. The elements she'd learned waiting for earth to have exchanged with sky the shivers of respective worth. Everything, eventually, was coming. With ripeness of an active verb attached to how she found her way to where and what she had become.

36.

He would not acknowledge green-lipped mussels on her plate. Sandwiches like threads. Milk following satiety. She said the urn negated thirst. It was his habit practically to unask. Beneath religion there was nothing to regret. Who presides over the finches. Extra credit roses beside the sack from Bloomingdale's. How to nourish reciprocity remained his search. *All forecast long he waited for ideas.* Something tickling easily remunerated something vast. *Why now* was all she asked to know. Shut things leave out vocals and in movies we are sentiment collectively. *Rock me in a stare* to trill without the instrument. Obsession with redemption naturally erases posture from the draft. How molten was his walk. How small and to the violets was his coasting. Damages promise slavery within repeat signs. Barometers uncross themselves. On tape she was without a brittleness of voice. Small built-in mercies link themselves to an economy. Floor lamps bought from Bea's on Indian School Road shed lather. Define for us a city. The string-drawn model plan that weaves and crosses weather and our prominence. Wood known to have fed saws. Saws known to have furnished context for a weather.

37.

Tangents bake themselves into our memory. What kind of rose requesting to be born where. Twist of the percussion that annihilated you last night. The sequined sacraments we offer modally. Many small descriptions lacking pomp are entryways to the profound. That's why she sold the collar with the dog that she was offering. Her partner phoned to tell me systems do not work where he's employed. What we talk about occurs in rows. An intimacy, not limited to who falls into bed. There is the bridging of the kinds of distances between concurrent rain and glaring sunlight, one of which instills a love of coffee. Sheet rock defines our house again. Fine powder that occurred when it was planted, salted aspects of the lungs. An afternoon constructed for advisement runs both cool and warm. My memories of being there are plush with the reality of what did not transpire. The oily flowers next to where we entered, advertise their lack of need for water. Someone define for me "indigenous," and I'll reclaim the attitude purloined on my arrival.

38.

Murmur something in a conversation as a sleeve echoes the skin. Like the mine of ivy waiting to be breast fed. Would a whisper (farmlight) obligate our first sensation privy to the nest. Be kind to what you own. Re-pose the question "Would you seek/accept this property" (a lower form of spouse). Say to self this litany or breach of confidentiality. This sliver of a seed allowed to flow. "The damages" (when plural) mean the bill. Four corners couched so spinely. Her litmus postcard acquiesced to shifted bias and lord-it-over showerprints. Coyness elongates or abbreviates. To change the thing itself redeems a kind of prowess from the public who declare what they have paid and keep on paying over time. The mendicants will never find soprano sense of humor and their signs will seem abrupt forever. Tenements the size of an imagination prompt some actor to be brave and say the lines. Admit what we are calling truth is truth. Not some fabricated misreality a phrase away from one who's fallen.

39.

Her law partner gifted the valet with an annuity,
having forgotten the correct amount to tip. The
financial markets offer comfort when the sand-
box has been rained upon. And air conditioning
invites amnesia to our headboards where we in a
way sleep slowly. Feasts erase the mime within
an audience perfection. There is no music like
blind heat to wade through in a biosphere. No
deletion comparable to lifesaving techniques. No
voice mail to touch. Licenses are plentiful until
you need one. Fudge factor, a useless snub of
duty. Incorrigible human beings used to be crip-
pled by the hurt tones of a mother's voice. Their
offspring whittle limbs for pleasure till they're
bored. There's no route of appeal. This woman
I'm supposed to find endearing but have never
met, isosceleses her young way across the land-
scape bearing gifts that should be hidden from
an able-bodied view. The air goes still to make
her breathing audible, to revive another morning
in a time I've labeled not my menstrual season.

40.

Easter morning pigeon eggshell broken into jagged halves. Nine thirty-three and several tasks in queue along the quadriceps of tithing illegalities. Promissory notes unbundle guilt from offerings. And fly-by evidence that we are not alone swathed in spring temperatures mid-city. Photostats connected by a strap of wheat. This aftermath of vigilance, an agitated gathering of muscles rarely in the mood. Morning, hypothetically a gift we like to care about instead of pounce on and consume. Impulse to stretch out, claim, breed, then exponentially acquire. Ransack whole nations that resist inducements to relax their doeskin jackets. Seat themselves with choreography intact. The bars encapsulating most zoo animals produce nostalgia in misunderstanding hearts. An Apollonian impulse to sever what is carved as rainbows sprawl across our line of sight. Held by a pair of eyes so tenderly as to connect a brow to sadness. Motion of predicted fruit trees offers nourishment at random for a population. Whose scholars overthink the few remaining options they recall.

41.

To seed a flue is likely to retrace a few wings with remaining culture in the background check. How many ways to iterate *nobody cares for acres of our lives.* Nobody saturates the lemon wedge with northern blessings. No one ripens like a touched cloud. Bake sales repeat themselves the way our matrilineal indulgence motions to a rumored self. Does downtime count or are we threaded with exact seams portioned in a curving window. Winking sentences is hard work. One cover charge resembles several of the rest. Chimes alone are dust. Valves reachable as homonyms occur to us, a lean quipped faction. Alacrity slims down its fist and reasons on. The limits of our wealth, defined as rafters. Seatmates clear a room when certain poses are achieved. The replete signs hasten to apprise our homeland of the slain availability of friends. Chants reform the background checks with gloves immaculate and soundproof. To fail a litmus test is to have choked on whole grain afternoons. Many separate days have learned to pass estrangement. Liquid coming from our row enoughs itself around contestants who will always homestead close to the amount saved on rhetorical indulgence.

42.

Features and benefits rolled off her tongue like
atmosphere she chanted back. The still life she
was thinking wrestled its emergency into a win-
dow seat where the original . . . *What is the real
cost of efficiency and how much does it damage
our hypotheses.* The wonder is our slide rule, how
it confiscates aluminum already stunned with
happiness. *A yeast-free remark may injure some-
one perfectly insensitive* became her theory, so
she watched what she might say. And tried to
track and teach the same until it stuck. The only
lie detector test that functions gushes in the
bloodstream. Others listen to the running water
of first blood extracting authenticity or find con-
nections ossified in their meandering. Cool wide
soft-positioned wings to best with navigating
every absence of a marking in the sky. Who
would have thought this modicum of justice
would betray our little village with its jaundiced
rules that satisfy until we hurt. The class of
those deciding coddles all the underclass who
think they rule. What matters is a feigned com-

munion satisfying those not fully aware although consumed.

43.

She listed other people's hobbies as arroyos while her own had buckled under petty sacrifice. Marbles that allegedly were lost tried to come home. Unwrinkled glass conversant with new principles unties mementos from an honor code. She tried to be my neighbor when I asked. This is each one's situation. Shared the way we lay down gravel to comprise a path. What sort of sandwiches are we to view in code when anyone who's worked is hungry. Latitude is scenic but we're new at this. And latitude is part-way bronzed immediately following the postwar news. Is any kind of wood an armful. Any kind of meteor the one we know. Remediation is the thing that makes digestion difficult. New forms of snow distract from settled moments trying on percentages of repartee. Barometers used to be free when we were iffy with our lawns. Some day she'll need me was the lore. And which of us will still be here.

44.

Tomorrow I will use both halves of my round trip ticket to hell. A mystiquectomy spurns prior power. To see Lucifer as merely plain is to remove all dazzle and mascara from the beast and start to radiate one's own. I will dip down with my immunity to discover what is tame. Sentence myself to light work inside the moat rings, ruminate about return on equity and real cost. I will ghost write the infernal scenery as a novice who believes herself a sun lamp. Not picturing ahead of time the faces. Relish severance like the annex birthright that it is. Be careful to retain the self sufficiency of my full adoration of the powers that stiffen, silken, structure me. The perfect seam of spine. Alertness that surrounds posture with tenderness, as preparation for a child.

45.

Keypad represents one-sided intercourse. Half
sleek black folder typifies the perfect pitch miss-
ing from childhood. *He mirrored his father's in-
ability to sing.* The choir director advocated
measuring the mouth open three fingers wide.
Practically no vocalist is suave by Tuesday's stan-
dards. I agree to formulate a document for pen-
nies. *She leaves papers on my desk she hesitates to
throw away.* This morning's news discussed our
study recently completed, referred to us as "a
private consultant." *Speak into the microphone.*
Impatience about justice turns bluebloods bluer
still. *Listen to rainfall narrate prospects in a life.
The norm will not continue to resemble what we
know today.* Dismal Midwestern afternoon all
hooded like crow's eyes. *One foot then the other.*
Not dance or miniature effects. Not parenting.
Not whole-toned paper. Just meet and confer
over thoughts no one will write about or tell.

46.

Something political can be impolite and prosperous. It can have scent with no fragrance projected. He was tall and thin, and is. Behind him, sky becomes irrelevant. Something immense in us arranges flowers for alleged fun. In childhood, he broke blooms at the stemtop and presented this soft armload. Which was the mistake . . . desiring them or easily forgiving. Now his narratives are nonexistent. Who of us likes stories that cannot include us. A speck of wind and all the petals gone. There is no need to repeat. Amber, a ritual we are trained to think is patience. He reported liking what he found himself repeating. Waxen they appeared, without the slightest hint of planning. Formed that way. Notice that we rarely say *requited*. Things don't have to be simple.

47.

A lemon is a car with someone driving. And the price of citrus fruit is rising. Relationships imperve some layers of ourselves. Sentences beseech us without people to propel them. His invitation if he meant one felt as smooth as red rocks do up close. Prayer to remedy this soon. At once the possibilities must overlap these sure intentions. Backstroking at top speed en route somewhere. The swell of overlap decides to haunt my sleep. I release each cold reflection like a sudden dream. The only rite I know is sung in alto voice by women sunned, and so dimensional that we might as well test out of trigonometry. No teacher capable of talk elects to teach such things. As people do not pay attention factually. They pant, they leave town, and they window shop throughout the shelf life of a winter clouded by another person's madness speaking languages we must profess never to know.

48.

Episodes untellable keep cropping the rest in our lives. I think to say one thing and sky obediently shapes itself to an inestimable blue because. The blimps seed by. Doors slam and rattle windows I possess with shades across them. The Vivaldi all perpetual simmers in this room where warmth costs. Night requires recovery I keep rehearsing until dream demands a second meeting. Negotiation with a spirit of one's own necessitates close reading. Memory might swerve. The mind divorced awhile from nature leaves its payments in a drawer projecting optimistic silence. Unsettled feeling between people may require more time to heal than an ocean as it shifts allegiance from one group of rocks to another. Pebbles become lozenges in the repeat breathing of seaslap across surfaces. As moonish as the sift of sky painted on glass doors that exist as much for neighbors as inhabitants.

49·

Strands of what I lived performed the breast stroke into the asylum he described. More sunny sides to this one street than anyone had claimed. Inextricable moves seemed grim at first then slightly curved. The two of us had meals and talked. The two of us would linger over small details we thought concerned us. Any day now crosses would begin to count. A little of the rpm we thought we'd lost on 45s is back to harm our psyches. Many furnaces are gemmed with stars. And many hemlines peaceably renege on deals ancestors made for us. *He seemed a brother meaning there was little sleeping to be done.* Betrayal is one person's hobby while reclining in a shrink's chair is the other's. How they belong together. Hours in the gymnasium elapse until we're fiery neat and chiseled fresh, unseeded. She would never blame him for his fondness of familiar solitude, having loved a man who'd won a prize that she would think was also hers.

50.

A missive prompted me to wash sea salt from windowpanes. I heard the hollering of gulls retiring in their Doppler gangs. Each century shook by to mean forethought had passed. The butternut attention beyond ripening would chant and then recede into the temples. Dark, alert to the arrival of oncoming glances. Some of the pictograph with shelled wings, runes and fishbones. A lobotomy of edifice. Economies all quivering with insolence belonging to the enemy. Removed from conscious earth as penitence has hovered easily. *Coming from a long line of investigative underlings who guide the mesh of trade and tribe,* at last the silo of a wing and mask and semiotic mentions till a cross is pried from hands with lust or hate in them. *To read these signals and these traced leaves.* Latency across from chosen shoulders, the too intrusive caring and the soft. Allowing puppetry to leave its bounds. Relive the self of first immersion that would last. Endow an other with the capability of casting song into a random sea and form a comfortable new gender with no name.

51.

Today's the Feast of Peetie Pie. The sweet palaver of her letters spelled percussion voice. Equally clover pencilled in rose lavender appointed spring. Who in our ancestral grace can smoothly function under pressure of a present tense. Line drive kisses fully wakeful lids. Appointments to the role we play return a serve. Impact internal flavors liked about ourselves. The ancillary flows fit muscles like a leotard. Greenhorns all light into a curious agreement between earth, flower, and earth again. A full moon pits encumbrance against breakdown in a smoother attitude. *Relax,* her spirit says to me, *the only avenue that matters is the lovespill you are slipping on. You're splendid in your own words. Small apostle brilliant as root cause. My validated harvest.*

52.

Nothing's an emergency at one. My goal's to move as many pages from my court as possible. Go to the health club, earn low fat. Define physique away from numbness, falling into connectivity without thought or intention. I want the universe to yield delicious accidents only my focused planning could have nudged. Chants possibly release us from our farthings. Mentionable equities enthrall us. Redemption is a part-time job, the vested shadows, summative. Delirium that comes from spring records a prophecy. Repeat dreams are for lingering around the impasse. Prompt beauty, most auspicious when refusing to let go. Cling peach expressive of frank summer wands. Likeness corralled in little pens we nickname foibles to the left of something as remarkable as not forgotten.

53.

One sacrament seems like the rest of these dull
blades. Remands are tripling in the nightbird fre-
quency apart from the undress of precipice. Un-
like our lymph nodes that require participation,
we accessibly receive symbolic mood rings. My
sentence calls for worthiness unhinged to wor-
thiness. A silhouette as gracious as a campsite
underlines my need for competence. The same
three recollections frame the same three then-
agains. If I were fearlessly a bird I'd window the
apartment east of what I wrote one time. I'd fin-
ish the last sundae. I'd retrieve in pigeon English
all the rumored toast, the province of so many
duckbills that the pond is skimmed impartially.
Encapsulate the Lenten sense of a falsetto puri-
ty. The only curfew in our midst seems head-
strong as the infant half of newlyweds. All mid-
night we'd been hoping for a safe place to reply.
A gravestone for deposit of unlikely souls. A min-
uet remaining in the repertoire as fast asleep as
scoliosis pending surgery. In my imaginary world
you might cost something to the tune of every al-

tercation dramatized. The mince meat we have used to scold supposed enemies assumes larval positions, leaking tiny penitentiaries almost as gold coast as these furnished wars. Streets completely full of us return our calls at the requested hour.

54.

She made better scenery than an alto flute. I had arranged to take the afternoon and fling it to off-duty shepherds oggling spring training in the park. Western amphitheatrics from hallways perjuring themselves. So everything that I recall of passion shows the relevance of cross hairs in the ready, aim of sanctioning. Tremendous pressure for a quiet landing spared the culture of interpretation. Catcalls emphasized unfinished plans. No known keyboard could handle the agility of music's furnishing a room of any kind. How personality reverses its outmodedness by playing with distraction, points of trust. Chess game defeative of the human. Resisted with a passion for removing rust before our time. A warble of her otherwise soprano making. Consonant with twist of lime to lift the drink above default vibrato of the middle fizz.

55.

Homonyms are just as pretty as their brothers. I have promised her the round and she's selected the rectangular again. I hear this smothering softer than floorboard squeak when she feels much too loved to have been forty. In a tiny room her shoulders partly sag. The projector rarely works. She has intended (is the story) to reveal small squares of lives in rapid sequence all prepared to be her past. The couch has cat hairs and the incense masks the house smell. With the window open who might notice. How often in the desert do we think about a lake. What is the function of white paint on white canvas.

56.

Threads accumulate touchprints connected to the light. So many fathoms deep. Strong spears gather from retention pending dust. As macro as the furred loop, eighty hours past erasure. When we argue, we are sugared. When we blush. When we elope to Kansas. Phantom characters exude charisma certainly. A long shore finally distracts from the osmosis pained in the direction of a hybrid west. Where demanding sequiturs derange the pulse that safens when it's heard, touched, felt. Placemats easily configure chain link tangents. Luminous retreats to majesty and barren traps with houses planted in them. As seniority impounds the only motor without scars. Exonerate the drip mode and relax into a watchful correspondence.

She prayed intimacy would dry and she'd be caught, fed, cared for in her own womb near the shiver of a half glanced moon. Symptomatic of a spun momentum forecast to mean penitence as inabrupt as anything afar. She ordered a decaffeinated merger of her lean intentions and the flat demands of love. The magazines untangled some of what had worried her. A simple prominence of gold shards webbed their way to purviews anyone had left unguessed. The only episode of passion seemed a shallow film to neighbors now invested in the recommended flings. As supple as her conversation was, it lacked assembly and deliverance. As cloistered as her obligation seemed, she delved into a weed pile till the southerly intact posh light commanded due respect. How do you tell a sibling that you've loved her shadow often. All the things there were to say came home to have been wooed again by loving manners. Telltale shapes return to what we think in colors brilliant to trained eyes. How many clothespins do we watch and why are they peculiar to our vision as we notice living rows be seeded toward completion.

58.

These walls purposely unpainted that I'm supposed to wish were down are welcome to my breastbone, welcome to my sleep. He's read the fable purpling white skin as mutuality. Presentenced walls. I press forms into his alibi, a hometown milk. Trend toward deepening a supposition that we bridge across. Having met late in the thickness of these walls. Would future promulgate a wrinkled violence ledged in his eyes. Sentences that prove apart these inclinations. Phrase from someone else's mouth or fastened to embedded cold a whistle past indulgences. Locus of selves practiced in the leaving out of connectivity to certain atmosphere. A necessary Braille, fine line between affection and the desperate claiming. Opposite of knee jerk, opposite of solo.

59.

Al fresco meeting in the morning, sevenish because the rented building did not come with extra key. Thread of time passed and a vehicle off-ramped its way into the parking lot with forty-five onlookers not quite shivering. Her tiny speech, "A good thing I'm here early," was the quickest on-your-feet protective marketing I'd seen. *People make different decisions when they're cold.* The degree to which a group is willing to be led astounds. *The crowd will genuflect or pay if information's given forcefully enough.* Who breaks a tie if the alternative is just as good. Bless the blessing of these birds, tunes not in traction. What does it take to world the rifle, out of consciousness. These birds exactly. Or being on assignment in the furniture showroom where plush amplitude is offered without clutter of emotion, coffee rings, or personalities. Have prayer accumulate in form of sight that rinses cloth and blood and evocation battered by pink light. The body needs a remedy for bodying. Muscle tone wants chair with seasoned flesh. *In passing, he reminded us of the importance of in-tention, application, and appreciation of a day.* The alterations lady is sequestered in a century no longer offered. How pretty resentment grew when oil in sunlight rainbowed what was merely puddle.

60.

Whatever age you are repeats itself in beauty
staged to meet meticulous requirements. As free
to take my meaning east as damages are carried.
Sanctions we would leave alone prefer them-
selves to be as tempting as the gathering of hints
you see and don't concurrently. *She called to tell
me something funny to distract me from her
breach of duty.* Bountiful address systems remove
themselves from thought when we are looking to
be tidy, candid, rapt. *I wouldn't say this to a soul,*
but do you know what he *consumes?* Whatever
the recipient is told to do she does perfumily
with arms crossed, legs crossed, heart apart from
intellect. Temptation the line drawing confis-
cates intention that had prompted it. Whenever
you have posed, you're saying to participants that
format of intention scapegoats all the polished
tables in the house. *How am I going to get out of
here* she asked herself. He needed every shred of
her attention as a fraction of his large portfolio.
He needed to have living wood become his furni-
ture. He needed most of all to sit and read the

lines and translate them to body lore that he might share with her if she'd consider a return.

61.

Attention forecasts clumsily swift winter's frost and shale and tread. The customer is crescenting a little trespass cold and trembling. Plow so temperate we skill our way toward brownstone after brownstone, chemistry intact. Mellifluous intent repeats our minds one plot point at a time. A courier awaits. Her shoes metallic pink and maybe sheer. The Valley is not pure again. Amendments code the line of sight. How many trickles of this money might be gobbled, whiplashed, or inferred. Aggressive growth funds titillate our Guernseys any road you take. Voice mail bearing slim resemblance to the moot point sinks to vigor. She talks incessantly in code until I dramatize what also works. The sheaves as foremost gray are tamed beside the rush. Alertness stemming from discomfort. Signal when you might be listening. I'll replace the old recording with some furniture drawn past the fever rumored to have linked us. While we lifted possibilities from quicksand not the same as city park. Leisure was presumed our legacy until the economic code began to rhyme with "bother" and we had to uproot our ancestry. Fine old groves susceptible to ruin, look their best awhile until photographers decide to leave and what is feared seems fated.

62.

Vigil enhopes our routine breathing to a focus. Otherwise, we classify arrangements toggled between pretty and not. Some domiciles require an ease that would make possible the kind of ingenuity most people do not even read about. Some domiciles require chaos to ensure feelings of usefulness by one of the inhabitants who might as well be furniture if not for the excruciating swirl. Crisp atmosphere with light all through it. Neighbor is vapid for the lack of liquid intake. We try to persuade her to accept a ginger ale. We try to persuade her to nudge the half-retired doctor to accept her in the hospital. The profit sector asks oceans of its victims. And we live where it is perfectly skin dry. We pray for our neighbor's life. She cannot hear us love her. Cannot hear the birds outside her window. Cannot hear the sirens of the ambulance that will carry her to safety. We take her mail upstairs. We take ginger ale. Take vegetable juice. The conversation, more a whisper than a strong call, hastens fear again. Prescription takes some hours to be called in by the confused physician. Who scolds to reveal affection which our neighbor takes as how things ought to be. No diagnostics are applied. One thing about the movies we have not seen: they mellow the mind cave. Make more palatable the progression of required events. Professionals may be rewarded for introducing the right questions. What about this house gives greatest comfort. The few spare photographs of people we include within our sphere of selves.

63.

He projected me into a quivering that lacked rigor. Then *fastened on erasure of a sweetness that he thought I saw* throughout the random winter. Prayer not different in his mind from tulips gathered accidental instances of growth (after the bulbs' tasting of soil). He snipped off contact, silverfine black thread accommodating shorter distances between us *with habit systems etched into established space*. Precision the memento carved initials in a tepid looking block, *foundation of his house* . . . no house of mine, lacking in wallspace and continuance. I did not promise to omit the beauty key or to earn realism that he might confer me. Whatever sifts its way through blinds of the selection process trembled a bouquet. Quenched by ideas of lunations as we learned them.

64.

Mingle different colored collars and you quash
this kind of sense nicknamed conveniently not
common. She liked things in a row. She could
pontificate about its various ingredients. There
were covert snobs hobnobbing in a park named
for Midwestern roots. The oleanders free played
their gnarled fingers as peached apprentices
glad-handed their way into the hearts of theory.
Palms needed to be shaved to life, pigeons shift-
ed to new quarters. The hamstring accidents re-
quire documentation. Then we'll all know where
we were. We'll all apparently be numb or we'll
crash course our way to the tribunal on the left.
It has grown noticeable people use *anxious* in-
stead of *eager* when they really have no fear at
all. Seat time climbs into the back reciting all
the ills experienced before the shrill balloon
shed deafness. We wanted to have courage but
we left our light behind. We wanted to defray
the cost of water and we wanted to call stillness
a commodity. All that remained of living sham-
rocks were appreciation and a photograph.

65.

He catalogues this puzzle slice that I'm supposed
to miss when faced with artwork partially invest-
ed in integrity. Ballet prevails, is my response. He
is listening to control issues rumored to be sen-
sual. Enough to lose potential tedium. This wash
of otherness has merely crayoned in its last name
stroke by fevered stroke. The modest apple pie of
sleep increases shelflife to reflect nest status one
could chronicle and give away. To bask in power,
a reflected form of crust. Restless, feasible, em-
phatic seedling someone might prefer. A violin or
malted blasphemed like a record. Slanted socks
entirely parted from the gentlest skin. One temp-
tation efficacious as the rest. A practicum dis-
guised as fossil bares its tool kit to descendants.
Crumb by crumb elected to be thumbing half a
ride to places cleats revise. What could someone
want with branches of this tree. A hammock
tempered with erased applause allows the body
to distemper kiss-lengthed fixtures sought to
mute lividity. Pumice jabbed turns powder in the
quilted hand. Sandpaper justice coins a phrase

tipped feasily a wink to western things. How many ought to fling their customs at a guard rail. Sideburns matter in a photograph. One chemistry as plausible as coughing spell. She pampers her digestive system or refrains and then regrets. Which cells comprise your audience. The film described as brisk. En route to clean air noted in advertisements conferring honors on improbable restraint. Allegro moderato stills monopolies as fanciful as sugar spun like fiberglass although consumed.

66.

Devotion is inverted crime. The way she finger-prints reality, I fear I will mistake this overlay with repeat business, the kind that's left in combs. I tell her something that remains in memory too long to be viable. She's still referring to it mindlights later. Rather than dismiss what she has made, I play with it a while, believing that my only perk is to squeak pilgrims of good-will from truthless rumors. One day she is singing and the next day she is stung in her re-gret. One day she is picturing amendments and the next she has unbranched whole forests next to me. I pantomime some moment at the office where they take me literally. So I am not afraid to talk. No echo machine blares out the substance of some fidgeting gray lie. She uses truth as an emollient or as collateral. I can't tell where my boundaries aren't. Commission anyone to draw some freehand. I'll obey. Just to have rituals. Just to have markings that I might respect. Just to know when I am finished trying to erase them.

GREEN INTEGER
Pataphysics and Pedantry

Douglas Messerli, *Publisher*

Essays, Manifestos, Statements, Speeches, Maxims,
Epistles, Diaristic Notes, Narratives, Natural Histories,
Poems, Plays, Performances, Ramblings, Revelations
and all such ephemera as may appear necessary
to bring society into a slight tremolo of confusion
and fright at least.

*

Green Integer Books